# PRELUDE TO THE SOUL

# VRITI

To my dearest friend, whose presence has been a constant melody in the symphony of my life. You are the quiet strength in my moments of doubt, the laughter in my silence, and the light that guides me through my darkest days. This book is a reflection of the bond we share a bond built on shared dreams, whispered secrets, and the unspoken understanding that needs no words. Thank you for being my muse, my confidant, and the heartbeat of my journey. May this work be a small token of the immense gratitude I feel for having you by my side.

With all my love,

Me

# Contents

# Preface

In a world brimming with activity, poetry offers a quiet sanctuary where emotions find rhythm and thoughts take flight. Prelude to the Soul is a journey through the many facets of the human spirit, exploring longing and fulfillment, despair and hope, solitude and connection.

Each poem is a window into the heart and mind, inviting reflection and rediscovery of beauty within and around us. Like a musical prelude, this collection seeks to awaken and stir something profound, offering not answers but illumination along life's path.

May these words inspire clarity, connection, and resonance with the shared journey of the soul.

With gratitude,

Vriti

# Prologue

The soul is a vast and mysterious ocean, its depths teeming with currents of thought, emotion, and memory. It is here, in the boundless expanse of our inner world, that poetry finds its truest home.

Prelude to the Soul begins with an invitation a beckoning to step into the unknown, to wander along the shoreline where the tangible meets the infinite. These poems are not merely words arranged with care; they are vessels of feeling, carrying fragments of the human experience across the waters of time and understanding.

In this collection, each verse serves as both a reflection and a mirror, offering glimpses of the universal through the deeply personal. Here, love whispers its truths, loss speaks its wisdom, and hope casts its light upon the shadowed path. These are the moments that shape us, the stories we carry in silence, the questions that linger unanswered.

The prologue is not an end but a beginning. It is a pause before the first step, a breath before the melody. As you embark on this poetic journey, allow yourself to linger in its silences, to hear the echoes of your own soul within its lines. For in the act of reading, we become not just witnesses but participants in the dance of words and meanings.

May this prologue awaken a curiosity within you to seek, to feel, and to dream. May it open the door to a realm where the soul speaks in whispers, and the heart finds its voice in verse.

PROLOGUE

Welcome to Prelude to the Soul. The journey awaits.

# Resurgence

In the pursuit of your best self,

A journey unfolds, seemingly tough.

Doubts and whispers may cloud your mind,

But resist the allure to surrender.

Keep pushing forward, stay aligned,

And the fruits of your efforts will render.

Struggles will rise, flames so fierce,

Threatening to consume your will.

With strength and resilience, you'll pierce,

Through the obstacles, your purpose fulfilled.

The heat of battle may seem unbearable,

But trust me, it's a refining fire.

For within the struggle, your growth is wearable,

And the outcome will exceed your deepest desire.

So, press on through every challenge faced,

With unwavering faith in your quest.

For in the end, triumph will be embraced,

And you'll realize it was all for the best.

The journey may seem daunting, it's true,

But the rewards will prove their worth.

As your best version comes into view,

You'll see that the journey gave birth,

To strength, wisdom, and self-discovery,

To resilience and unyielding might.

For in the face of adversity,

You bloomed, shining ever so bright.

So, my dear, hold on and endure,

The journey to your best self.

For when you reach the end, you'll be sure,

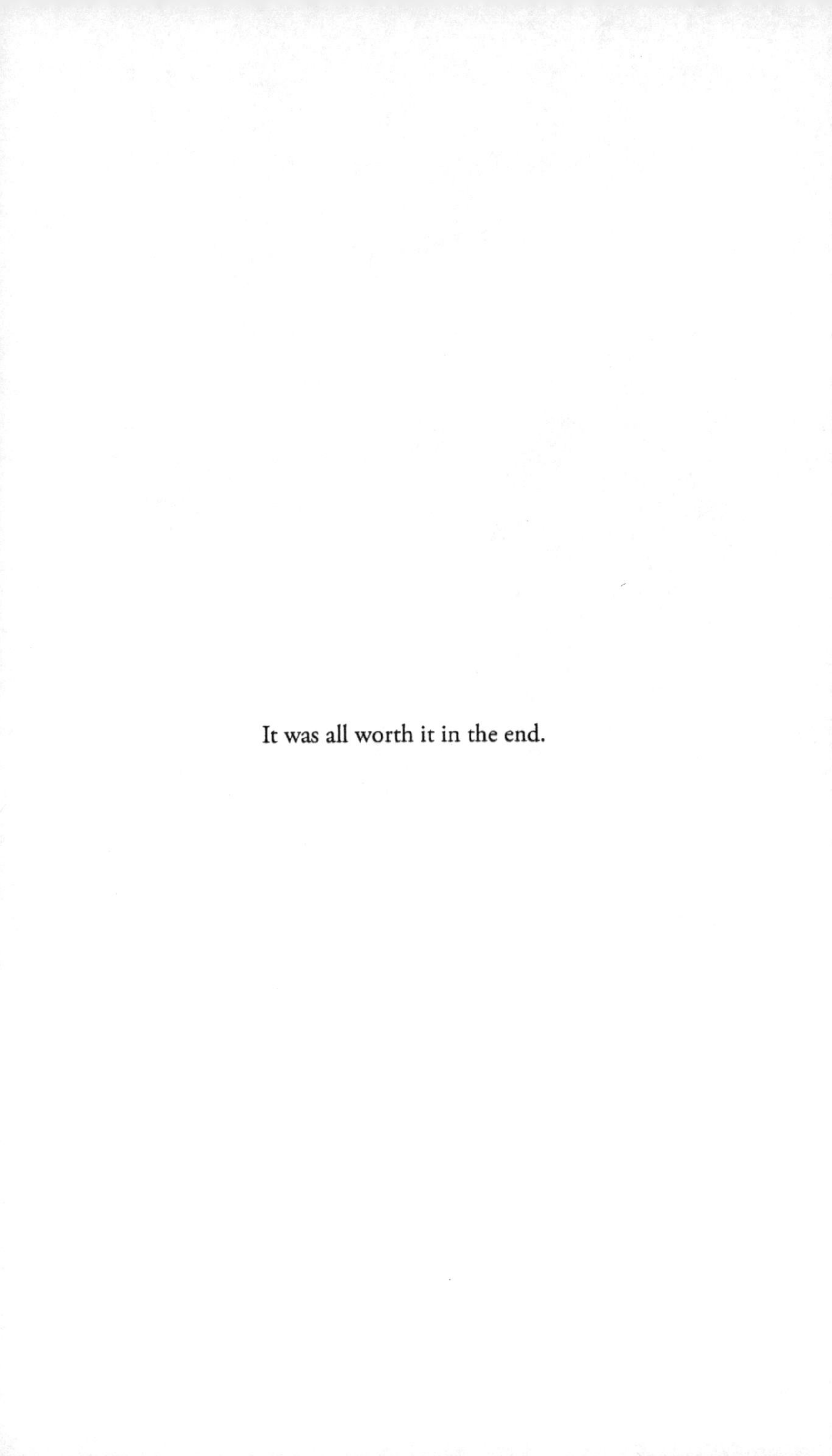

It was all worth it in the end.

# We all live out of boxes

Life's boxes, we hold them near,

Some from need, some from fear.

We think they make us whole and sound,

Yet in this cycle, truths are found.

We say we can't live without a box,

In attachment's grip, we're tied like knots.

But when one's gone, we search for more,

Inventories filled, as before.

We call each other selfish, it's true,

But miss the self within, in our view.

Till one day, time takes our own,

Our box vanishes, and we're alone...

# Shadow's Light

In the depths of your heart,

Where shadows reside,

Lies the key to illuminate,

To let light inside.

Journey to the darkness,

Embrace the unknown,

For in the blackest night,

A brighter path is shown.

Like a dark spot on white,

Drawing your gaze,

It beckons you closer, through life's maze.

Embrace the contrast,

The beauty in strife,

For only through darkness,

We cherish the light of life.

# It feels like Love

Still! everything around.

Let the silence fill me up,

With all that went unnoticed,

Unappreciated in the noise

That surrounds me.

Let the thumping sound of my heart,

Be the only noise that flows inside me,

And let me meet myself today,

To share how I have been.

Let the darkness be at its best as I close my eyes,

And dwell inside to see if some light is left.

Let the only perfume that I smell today,

Be the fragrance of my aura,

For I wish to fill myself with its freshness yet again.

Let me kiss my broken self and heal the wounds,

Cause it feels like love!

# A Bond of Light

Two souls stand together, a radiant pair,

One adorned in gold, glowing beyond compare.

Her laughter shines like the morning sun,

A melody of joy where hearts are won.

Beside her, calm, with a starry grace,

A quiet strength etched upon her face.

Her short, soft hair, like whispers of night,

Holds a charm serene, yet burning bright.

Together, they bloom like day meets dusk,

A friendship sweet no need for musk.

One, the fire, ablaze with cheer;

The other, the moon, steadfast and near.

Through life's dances, through its art,

They carry each other, heart to heart.

In golden hues and midnight's gleam,

They build together their cherished dream.

A picture of love, a story untold:

Two girls, one bond, more precious than gold.

In their union, the world may see

The essence of friendship, pure and free.

# Till We Meet Next

Till we meet next, beneath the moon's gaze,

I'll trace your absence through shadowed haze.

Your touch a ghost in the midnight air,

A silent ache, a tender despair.

Till we meet next, when time bends and breaks,

I'll count each moment the heartache makes.

A love so deep, it defies the stars,

Yet lingers here with its quiet scars.

Till we meet next, in some far-off dream,

Where nothing is lost and all is as it seems,

I'll wait for you through the endless night

My heart your beacon, my soul your light.

# Life never met me

Life never met me but asked me to live.

With unseen hands, it gently did give,

A path to wander, a story to weave,

A journey unknown, yet asked me to believe.

Life never met me but offered a chance,

To dance with the shadows, to join in the dance.

It spoke in the sunsets, in the rustling leaves,

In the heart's deepest yearnings,

In the dreams one conceives.

Life never met me but asked me to be,

A part of its wonder, a drop in its sea.

In every heartbeat, in every breath,

It whispered of living beyond fear of death.

But life never met me…

# Where the stars feel like home

Standing in silence, looking at the stars,

Some bright, some dim, like whispers from afar.

Clouds taking a walk, kissing the bright white moon,

Then drifting away, leaving night in a silvered swoon.

I see all this, and I feel like home,

Beneath the vast sky, where my heart can roam.

In the dance of the heavens, in the soft, gentle glow,

I find a peace, a place I always know.

# Threads of Unbreakable Friendship

Best friends know every little curve and turn of your life,

Navigating moments of low and high, joy and strife.

They understand when to hold your hand, gentle and light,

And when to hug you tight in the dead of night.

In the tapestry of time, they weave their love so fine,

Stitching together hearts with an unspoken line.

Their presence is a balm, a whispered, steady guide.

Best friends, the real ones, will strive to be by your side.

Through the storms that rage and the sunshine so bright,

They anchor your soul, making everything right.

In the silence, in the laughter, they remain your light.

Best friends, the real ones, hold on with all their might.

# The Quite Leak of the Heart

It didn't break, but there was a crack,

A silent fissure, a subtle attack.

What leaked from it, unseen, untamed,

Were emotions never reached, never named.

Whispers of sorrow, echoes of dreams,

Silent currents in hidden streams.

The heart's reservoir, once so strong,

Now seeps with feelings, silent and long.

No shattering sound, no grand reveal,

Just a slow release, a quiet appeal.

Unspoken words, in the darkness trapped,

Now slowly flowing, their silence unwrapped.

In the stillness, the quiet sighs,

Emotions drift like soft goodbyes.

They touch the air, then fade away,

Lost to the world by night and day.

Yet in the leak, there lies a grace,

A gentle softness, a tender space.

For though unspoken, they still exist,

These fragile feelings, like morning mist.

They reach no ears, they find no rest,

But in the heart, they still invest.

A silent story, a muted song,

Of a love enduring, deep and strong.

# Dancing in the Downpour

Not all the rains are meant for you,

Few will leave you dry for a lifetime.

Lost in a flood of tears,

Drowning in the echoes of goodbye.

Each drop a reminder of the love

We once knew, now gone.

I stand in the storm, shattered by memories,

Left to carry on alone.

So let the thunder roll,

Let the lightning strike,

I'll weather the storm,

Though it feels like I might break.

Not all the rains are meant for you,

Few will leave you dry for a lifetime.

But I'll dance in the downpour,

Until the clouds finally break…

# The Quiet Absence of Joy

Smiles are all around, but not on my face,

For you are not here, and I'm lost in this space.

Laughter echoes in the air, a joyous sound,

Yet my heart feels heavy, with you not around.

Sunlight dances, casting golden hues,

But my world feels Gray, shrouded in blues.

Flowers bloom, their beauty so profound,

Still, my soul aches, with you not around.

Moments pass, yet time seems to freeze.

In your absence, I'm left with just memories.

A sea of smiles, a crowd of cheer,

But my own smile fades, wishing you were near.

Dreams of us linger in the quiet of night,

Hoping one day you'll return and make things right.

Until then, I'll wait in this lonely place.

Smiles are all around, but not on my face...

# Whispers in the Language of the Heart

In the quiet of the night, when words fade away,

Talk to me; let your thoughts come out to play.

In the whispers of the wind, in the rustling leaves,

In the silence that conceals all that one perceives.

Share with me your dreams, your fears, your joys.

Let your voice be the music that my soul employs.

In a world so loud, so full of noise and haste,

Talking to you is like finding a peaceful place.

Through the highs and lows, the laughter and the tears,

Our conversations bloom like flowers through the years.

So talk to me, dear friend, in the language of the heart,

For in the art of speaking, true connections start.

# Where Souls Entwine

In your big, bright eyes, a fearless smile,

I find a love that's truly worthwhile.

Your touch, so docile, a gentle caress,

Bringing me joy, vanishing all distress.

Unsaid words between us, volumes they speak,

In the silence, our love reaches its peak.

I long to dive deeper into your heart,

Where our souls entwine, never to part.

With you by my side, I feel truly whole.

In your love, I've found my very soul.

Together, we'll journey, hand in hand,

Forever united in a love that'll stand.

# Illuminations in the Shadow

In the shadows of the night, we find our way.

Alone we walk, with burdens to sway.

Heavy is the weight we carry deep inside,

In each silent step, our fears we hide.

No one sees the struggle, the silent fight,

Only you and your creator, in the dark of night.

A journey known only to the heart and soul,

A path to understanding, to make us whole.

If awareness dawns, the end may near,

But if oblivious, the cycle begins clear.

Embrace the darkness; let it be your guide,

For within the night, your light will abide.

# Elegy of the dying Light

Upon the ocean's solemn song,

The sun descends; the day is gone.

A fading light, a somber sight,

As darkness falls, the waves unite.

The sea mirrors the fading glow,

A lonesome beauty, a heartfelt show.

Whispers of sorrow in the breeze,

Sunset and sea, an endless unease.

The horizon fades into night,

As the sun slips away from sight.

In this moment, aching and still,

The sea and sunset sing their bittersweet fill.

# The Echoes of a Lost Childhood

I wanted to grow and grow up fast,

To taste the freedom, a world so vast,

Where laughter sparkled in every hue,

And life was fresh and always new.

But as the years began to climb,

I lost those joys, one at a time,

The smiles, the ease, the simple days,

The friends and family, carefree ways.

The games we'd play, the endless fun,

All faded slowly, one by one.

And now I look back, filled with regret,

At days I wish I'd never forget.

Oh, if I could turn time's steady tide,

Hold close the child I keep inside.

To laugh, to play, without a care,

In moments light as summer air.

To be that child, with all my heart,

To hold that joy and never part.

# The Sacred Vow of Trust

Never break a trust, so deep and true,

From someone who gave their heart to you.

Their faith, a treasure, fragile, rare,

A bond that love and care declare.

In their eyes, you're a guiding light,

A beacon glowing in the night.

To hold that trust is to hold the sky,

A sacred vow, a whispered tie.

For when trust shatters, it leaves a scar,

A wound that lingers, near and far.

So, guard it well, with every part,

And honor the gift of a trusting heart.

# Did you know me from before?

Did you know me from before?

In a life, a time, a distant shore?

When echoes of the past were clear,

And shadows whispered, drawing near.

Did our paths entwine in days long gone,

Where memories linger, like an old song?

Did we share a glance, a word, a breath,

In moments untouched by time or death?

Perhaps we met beneath ancient skies,

Where the stars held secrets in their eyes.

Or maybe in dreams, where souls do soar

Did you know me from before?

In this life, this fleeting span,

I wonder if you're the same as then.

A spark, a face, a heart once more

Did you know me from before...

# The Endless Journey of Becoming

Every day, every moment,

There is something or someone

Flying away, far from us to never return.

Things, time, memories, people, all have a path,

A journey to leave a place and connect with something new.

We are all walking away from everything,

Every day, every moment, paths unfold,

As fleeting shadows dance and fade,

Leaving echoes of what once was whole.

In the silent spaces between breaths,

The whispers of departure softly call,

Guiding us to unknown realms,

Where yesterday's dreams dissolve and fall.

Yet, in this endless flow and flight,

We find ourselves anew each day,

Embracing change, the bittersweet,

As we walk away, yet somehow stay...

# Unbroken

She was quiet, but not short of words.

In her silence, stories unheard.

Wounded, but not scared at all,

She stood firm; she did not fall.

Tired, but not hopeless,

Her spirit soared, relentless.

Cornered, but not clueless,

Her mind sharp, resolute, and fearless.

She was betrayed, but still had trust,

In life's journey, adjust she must.

With a heart that knew both joy and pain,

She rose again, through the strain…

# Shadow's Light

In the depths of your heart,

Where shadows reside,

Lies the key to illuminate,

To let light inside.

Journey to the darkness,

Embrace the unknown,

For in the blackest night,

A brighter path is shown.

Like a dark spot on white,

Drawing your gaze,

It beckons you closer, through life's maze.

Embrace the contrast,

The beauty in strife,

For only through darkness,

We cherish the light of life.

About the Author

Vriti is a poet, dreamer, and seeker of meaning. Writing has been a lifelong passion, a way to navigate the complexities of life and to celebrate its beauty. When not immersed in the world of words, Vritti can be found sipping coffee and enjoying her favorite classical music. This is her first poetry collection.

Thank you for embarking on this journey through Prelude to the Soul. May the words linger long after the last page.

www.ingramcontent.com/pod-product-compliance
Lightning Source LLC
Chambersburg PA
CBHW020512160726